IMAGES
of America

WICHITA'S RIVERSIDE PARKS

IMAGES
of America

WICHITA'S
RIVERSIDE PARKS

James E. Mason

ARCADIA
PUBLISHING

Published by Arcadia Publishing
Charleston, South Carolina

Printed in the United States of America

Library of Congress Control Number: 2010931803

For all general information, please contact Arcadia Publishing:
Telephone 843-853-2070
Fax 843-853-0044
E-mail sales@arcadiapublishing.com
For customer service and orders:
Toll-Free 1-888-313-2665

Visit us on the Internet at www.arcadiapublishing.com

Dr. Edward Tihen read every issue of the *Wichita Eagle* and *Wichita Beacon* from 1872 to 1982 and wrote down the significant local events the papers reported, along with the day, date, and page number the articles appeared on. A Riverside resident, he made particular note of what happened there. Tihen's notes were donated to the Special Collections Archives at the Wichita State University Library. They have been transcribed by the library's staff and can be accessed through the Internet. This book would not have been possible without them. (Courtesy Wichita/Sedgwick County Historical Museum.)

CONTENTS

Acknowledgments   6

Introduction   7

1.   Shuman's Grove, the First Riverside Park   11

2.   Davidson's Park Becomes Riverside Park   19

3.   Three Riverside Parks   27

4.   The Zoo in Riverside Park   37

5.   Historical Features in the Riverside Parks   57

6.   The Other Riverside Parks   73

7.   Recent Times in the Riverside Parks   105

Bibliography   126

Index   127

ACKNOWLEDGMENTS

As a naturalist, I might seem to be the wrong person to produce an urban history book. But my experience with observing natural landscapes and how their present appearance results from past changes was good practice in researching my hometown. Having worked in Riverside Park for over 30 years, I saw traces of the past around me and wondered how they came to be.

Many people have assisted me in my search for park history. Bill Ellington, the former Wichita city historian, offered many valuable pointers when I began my investigations over 20 years ago. The large collection of materials he put together during his tenure at the local history section of the Wichita Public Library is an enduring legacy of his passion for the past. The current city historian, Michelle Enke, showed me how to browse the collection and pulled numerous photographs from the archive for this book.

Jami Frazier Tracy at the Wichita-Sedgwick County Historical Museum was very helpful in accessing their collections. The current director of the museum, Eric Cale, and his predecessor, Bill Puckett, have both cheered this project on.

Mary Nelson, program consultant with the Special Collections and University Archives at Wichita State University Libraries, found some unique photographs of the parks that I had never seen before, but had hoped to. Deborah Dimmick at Exploration Place took time from her schedule to unpack stored materials from their Grand Opening display. Mike Hutmacher of the *Wichita Eagle* provided access to their photographic archive. Susan Miner reviewed an early draft of this book and offered both valuable suggestions and encouragement. Kent Carter and Greg Hissem graciously shared photographs and materials from each of their family's past.

Lastly, I would like to commend all those people over the decades that could have thrown away the photographs and artifacts shown herein, but didn't. You did the right thing.

Except where otherwise stated, all photographs are taken from the author's private collection.

INTRODUCTION

During the Civil War, members of a tribe known as the Wichita were living in Indian Territory (Oklahoma) and facing persecution because they were sympathetic to the Union. For their protection, they moved north into their former homeland in the south central region of Kansas. They chose to live near the junction of the Arkansas and Little Arkansas Rivers in an area of Wichita now called Riverside.

The Wichita were relocated back to Indian Territory after the war, but the white traders and merchants who had come to the area because of the Indian trade remained and began a new town, which they named for the tribe that had lived there. The city of Wichita grew initially on the Indian trade, then prospered from the brief era of open range cattle drives, eventually becoming a market center for the abundant agricultural production of the area.

The rivers that had brought people to the site were largely ignored as a place of recreation at first. The fish in the rivers were exploited for food, and the riverbanks were used as dumping grounds for any and all refuse. Most homes and businesses were not built close to the rivers because of the periodic floods, which helped preserve the land next to them as open space. Eventually, though, the rivers and the wooded areas along them were recognized for the scenic beauty they offered in an otherwise treeless prairie, and efforts were made to turn them into parks.

The area near the junction of the two rivers, now known as South Riverside Park, was the first place to be called Riverside Park, but it did not get that name until 1883. Until then, it was known as Shuman's Park (or Shuman's Grove), and many chose to keep calling it that even though it acquired three other names over the next two decades.

In 1886, sixteen years after Wichita's founding, the wedge of land between the Arkansas and Little Arkansas Rivers had no bridge access and was still hard to get to. Some of it was being farmed, but it was otherwise a mixture of woodlands, pastures, and sandy hummocks created by the meanderings of the rivers over the centuries. About this time, a group of speculators formed the Riverside Land Company and drew up plans to develop part of the land between the rivers as an elegant suburban residential area. They acquired the property and submitted their plat document for the Riverside Addition on May 26, 1886. In the plat, the area now known as Central Riverside Park was marked as a reserve, not divided into house lots. The outline of what would become one of the largest, most scenic and beloved parks in Wichita was inscribed on vellum from the outset.

To make their venture a success, access across the river was essential. The Riverside investors built an iron truss bridge at Oak Street, which was opened on May 13, 1886, as a free public bridge. They also incorporated a streetcar line to connect Riverside with downtown Wichita. The line used electric cars, a brand-new innovation.

Amenities were added to the new park, most prominent of which was a half-mile racetrack oval angled from southwest to northeast. Other amenities included a 150-foot-long horse stable, benches, a bowling alley, picnic facilities, a dance platform, a concert pavilion, and playground equipment. Along the edge of the river, teams of laborers with horses and wagons leveled out the banks and built a boulevard along the now-smooth perimeter, adding a scenic drive overlooking the river to the list of attractions. Local investor J. O. Davidson was prominent in the Riverside Land Company, and the park became known as Davidson's Park.

Meanwhile, the South Riverside Park acreage was bought in 1893 by Frank Griswold, an impresario from Willoughby, Ohio, who was nationally known for his traveling theatrical production of *Uncle Tom's Cabin*. He failed to make the park self-supporting and defaulted on the loan only two years later. The bank that held the note in turn went under, and the county ended up owning the land. After a prolonged squabble over terms, the county finally sold the land to the city for $5,000 in February 1899.

After a very bright beginning, the Riverside Addition faded when the local land speculation boom went bust, followed by the national economic depression of the early 1890s. The Oak Street Bridge was sold to the city in 1890 for $4,000. The Riverside Land Company was liquidated, and ownership of its property transferred to a New England trust, the Keene Syndicate. This set the stage for the creation of public parks on the formerly private land.

The notion of public ownership of the land that would become the Riverside Parks was not new. City officials had visited the area on June 26, 1889, and had favorably discussed the idea of converting what was then called Shuman's Park (South Riverside), Davidson's Park (Central Riverside), and Greiffenstein's Park (North Riverside) to public ownership. In 1890, the city council proposed to float a bond issue for purchasing the land, but the hard times prevented them from following through.

Things improved towards the end of the decade. Mayor Finlay Ross and Councilman Ben McLean orchestrated a $14,000 bond issue for park creation that was overwhelmingly approved by the voters on November 2, 1897. Of that sum, $10,600 was used to purchase 106 acres at $100 per acre. The remaining $3,400 was used to add amenities to the park and build two new bridges to improve access to the area. Thus, Davidson's Park became the heart of the Riverside Parks System.

Initially improvements within the new parks emphasized landscaping. Numerous flower beds were created, mostly around a new central focal feature of the racetrack oval and on two new walkways the city added that bisected the oval lengthwise and widthwise. The sandy soil and summer heat made it difficult to maintain these beds, and the park staff took great pride in what they were able to accomplish. Evergreen trees were planted around the racetrack oval, walkways, and drives extant at the time. Several of those trees still survive today, indicating where the drives and walkways were once located.

In 1900, people started talking about displaying some animals in the park. Pens were constructed near the Woodman Bridge, and the Riverside Park Zoo was established. The first species kept were native, which included whitetail deer, elk, and pronghorn. The zoo immediately became very popular and grew. By the end of 1910, it had 172 animals ranging from doves to bison displayed in numerous cages and pens, as well as a large concrete waterfowl pond.

In 1910, the zoo acquired three alligators that would live there for 62 years. A concession stand in the form of a Japanese pagoda was erected the following year. In 1912, a central animal house, the Park Zoo, was added. It was only one wing of a proposed larger building that was never constructed, but it was a substantial improvement to the zoo nonetheless.

At the same time interest in the parks increased, so did the number of automobiles. Pedestrians and horse-drawn buggies had formerly wandered freely around the zoo area, but the advent of cars created congestion and conflict. In the early 1920s, streets were created through the park to segregate and confine the car traffic. The growth of automobile traffic caused many changes, not only in the parks but throughout the city. Horses were rapidly disappearing from Wichita streets. The streetcars were still busy, but usage began declining, and the last streetcar line would cease operation in 1935.

The Riverside Parks are the heart of the Wichita park system, but many other parks, both public and private, have been located along the rivers in the city. In 1905, shortly after the inception of the Riverside Parks, a large island in the middle of the Arkansas River known as Ackerman's Island was developed as a private amusement park. Wonderland Park had a skating rink, theater, indoor swimming pool, and what was touted as the largest roller coaster in the Unites States. People could reach the island via streetcar over a bridge specially built for the purpose. Due to restrictive blue laws that prevented charging admission on Sundays, Wonderland Park closed in 1917.

On the south end of the island, a baseball stadium was constructed in 1912. Amateur and semi-pro games were held there until 1933. A balloon race lifted off from the infield one day in 1915, and the winner landed in northern Arkansas the next. Articles about the race ran in newspapers nationwide. The stadium was torn down in 1933, and the island itself was removed as a public works project the following winter by hundreds of men, working only with shovels and wheelbarrows.

A dam was built on the Little Arkansas River above Wichita in 1874 to provide water for a mill in the east part of town. Forty years later, the impounded water above the dam became a local summertime resort known as Walnut Grove. Wichita's first air show was held there in 1911, with hundreds of people turning out to watch the new-fangled airplanes take to the sky.

The first downtown dam on the Little River was built in 1894, and another was built a short distance upstream in 1898. These dams made the Little River an outstanding place for recreational boating, which exploded in popularity; however, boating was popular on it even before the dams were built. The last mile or so before the river joined the Arkansas was a deep, fairly wide channel, just right for an afternoon outing in a rowboat. W. C. Woodman built a home in 1874 on the east bank of the Little River he called Lakeside, in reference to the appearance of the river at that point. Boating became vastly more popular once the dams made the body of water even wider and extended it further upstream, resulting in businesses setting up shop up to meet the demand.

In 1911, a public swimming hole called the Municipal Beach was created on the Little River in South Riverside Park. Four years later, it moved upstream on the north bank of the river, and a concert stage was added nearby in 1918. In 1923, a huge concrete swimming pool was built in South Riverside Park, which retained the name Municipal Beach. It was rebuilt in 1938 and served until 1969, when it was removed.

In 1922, a larger bear pen and a tropical house for exotic plants and birds were added to the zoo. The Park Zoo was replaced with an improved building in 1927. It was referred to as both the "Lion House" and "Monkey House," as it contained both animals. The crest of the zoo's popularity came during the Great Depression, when it would sometimes draw a million visitors per year. In 1938, a man named Bernie Goodrum became the new director of recreation at the zoo. The memorable experiences the Goodrum family enjoyed during that time were the basis of a humorous memoir written 30 years later by Bernie Goodrum's son Charles.

By the 1960s, a new facility was needed, but a modern zoo required more space than was available in the park. This led to the creation of the Sedgwick County Zoo on land that was, at that time, at the edge of town. The large animals of the Riverside Zoo were sent elsewhere. The bear den and lion house were demolished in 1972, and the alligator pit was filled with earth and converted into a prairie dog display. Along with that display in 1973, two waterfowl ponds and an open-cage structure built in 1960 were all that was left.

Wichita celebrated its centennial with a year of special events that culminated in a festival on the Arkansas River in May 1970. That festival was such a success, it was developed into an annual 10-day event, the Wichita River Festival, which draws over 100,000 people every year. As the nation's bicentennial approached, plans were made to build a Native American cultural center downtown at the junction of the rivers. A monumental sculpture was created for the site, the *Keeper of the Plain*, which has become emblematic of Wichita.

While the Riverside Parks were often the focus for river festival events and continued to be used, development and improvement lagged. A few years after the big swimming pool was removed from South Riverside Park, a new tennis center was built. The Woodman Bridge was replaced in 1975. A disc golf course was installed in Oak Park. But Central and North Riverside Parks had nothing new added to them since the 1920s, and what features they did have were showing their age or had been removed altogether, such as the large animal exhibits at the zoo in 1972.

The remaining part of the zoo was replaced with a new facility in 1988. That transformation seemed to catalyze public interest in doing something new with the rest of the Riverside Parks. After many years of meetings and discussions, a plan was drawn for a comprehensive renovation. When capital improvement money became available, the plan was put into action from 2002 to 2004.

The streets through the middle of Central Riverside Park, which had been built in 1921 in response to the advent of automobiles, were removed to reclaim the heart of the park for pedestrians. New features were added to the park, some echoing what one could find in the park a hundred years before, yet some additions were entirely original. The water features and lagoons at Oak Park were refurbished, the landscaping around Park Villa was refurbished, and the Riverside Parks enjoyed a new beginning as they moved into the 21st century.

One

Shuman's Grove, the First Riverside Park

Approaching from the highlands to the east, trader and naturalist James R. Mead first encountered the Little Arkansas River in June 1863. Many years later, he wrote of the experience: "The Little Arkansas was a gem; a ribbon of stately trees winding down to the parent river through a broad, level valley of green . . . dotted over with the black bodies of fat, sleek buffalo and an occasional group of antelope or straggling elk, and not a living human soul in all the country now known as Sedgwick county."

James R. Mead came to Wichita in 1863 as a young man and became a successful Indian trader and was highly regarded as fair and honest by all those who dealt with him. He helped found the city and further prospered through investments in real estate and various businesses. He was also a pioneer naturalist, whose observations of the land and its wildlife are an invaluable record of pre-settlement Kansas. (Courtesy Wichita/Sedgwick County Historical Museum.)

The first buildings constructed at what would become Wichita were across the Little Arkansas River to the east of what is now Central Riverside Park. This painting of the settlement, as it appeared in 1869, was done by Wichita artist Coy Avon Seward in 1920. It was based on recollections of William Finn, Wichita's first surveyor. Structures seen here include the Munger House, Wichita's first saloon, and Durfee's Trading Post. (Courtesy Wichita/Sedgwick County Historical Museum.)

The First House in Wichita.
Built in 1868 by D. S. Munger, now part of the Conklin home
901 N. Waco Avenue
Copyright 1907 by Ira Minnich.

Darius Munger built a house in Wichita at what is now the northwest corner of Eighth Street and Waco Avenue. It served not only as a residence, but also as post office and hotel. It was incorporated into a larger house in 1873 by William C. Woodman and lay hidden for many years. It was severed from that structure in 1911 and moved a short distance west in the 1920s.

Darius Munger was co-founder of the city of Wichita. He and William Greiffenstein combined their town plats for Wichita at the federal land office in El Dorado, Kansas, in 1870. Munger's plat lay to the north, around the site of his cabin; Greiffenstein's lay to the south. The downtown eventually centered on Douglas Avenue in the south part, but the Riverside area was where Wichita began. (Courtesy Wichita/Sedgwick County Historical Museum.)

13

In 1941, this stone marker was placed at the west end of the Douglas Avenue Bridge to show where the Chisholm Cattle Trail originally crossed the Arkansas River. The Chisholm Trail was a major route used to bring Texas longhorns to railheads for shipment east, and Wichita's founders made sure the trail came there. The river divided what was considered the respectable east side of town from the rowdy west side.

The first bridge across the Arkansas River in Wichita was built at Douglas Avenue in 1872. It was a private toll bridge at first, but it was bought by combined city, county, and public subscription funds and converted to a free public bridge in 1877. While it was still a toll bridge, many chose to ford the river and avoid paying the toll when the water level was low. (Courtesy Wichita/Sedgwick County Historical Museum.)

1875

The first recorded river-related recreation in Wichita was during the cattle-drive era. In the summer of 1872, shortly after the Douglas Bridge was completed, saloon girls in the wild and wooly cow town of Delano on the west side of the Arkansas would strip, race each other to the river, and jump in. The cowboys would lay bets on the outcome, fire their pistols, and generally whoop it up. This was known as the "Race of the Amazons." Wichita responded by passing a law against bathing in the river, but it was only enforced during the daytime. This raucous era of west Wichita is celebrated in one of the four relief sculptures on the Delano clock tower in the traffic circle at Douglas Avenue and Sycamore Street.

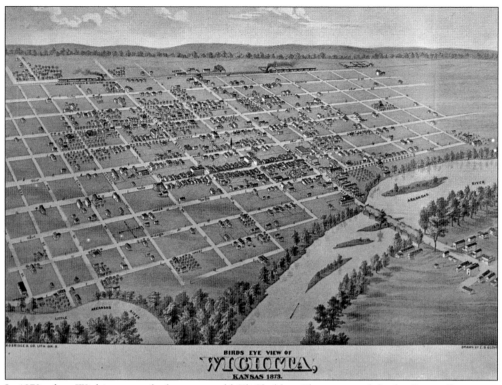

In 1873, when Wichita was only three years old, Eli Sheldon Glover created this bird's-eye illustration of the town as if viewed from the northwest. It was very detailed, showing every structure and even accurately depicting the eight spans of the Douglas Avenue Bridge. The junction of the two rivers is shown as a heavily wooded area. Only a few small islands are seen in the river. (Courtesy Wichita/Sedgwick County Historical Museum.)

This marker sits on the bank of the Little Arkansas River opposite South Riverside Park, near the Wichita Art Museum. It was placed there in 1982 by the Jane Peebles Sexton Chapter of the Daughters of the American Colonists to mark the spot where the two rivers once joined. A large island once stretched from the *Keeper of the Plains* west beyond Old Cowtown. Sim Park Drive follows the original riverbank.

South Riverside Park was the first of the Riverside Parks. It went through several owners prior to being acquired by the city in 1899. Each attempted to develop it as a place of recreation. Every time it changed hands, it gained a new name. At first it was Shuman's Grove (1872–1883) before becoming Hartzell's Park (1883–1884), Gay's Park (1884–1893), and finally Griswold's Park (1893–1895). John Wesley Hartzell named it Riverside in 1883. (Courtesy Wichita State University Library, Department of Special Collections.)

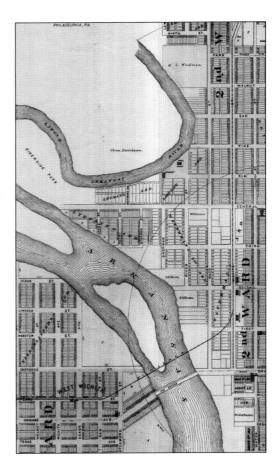

The Arkansas Valley Agricultural Society held its first three annual fairs in what is now South Riverside Park every September from 1880 to 1882. It moved the annual event to a new location west of the Arkansas River the following year. The rival Sedgwick County Agricultural Association was founded in 1872 and held its annual event on 40 acres located about a mile north near Seventeenth Street and Arkansas Avenue. (Courtesy Kansas State Historical Society.)

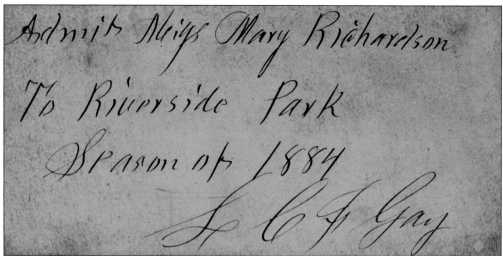

In an October 2, 1884, front-page newspaper advertisement in the *Wichita Eagle*, George and Lucy C. F. Gay proclaimed Riverside Park as the place for "Boating, Bathing and all sorts of Aquatic Sports." There were also "Merry-Go-Rounds, Swings, Croquet, Gymnasia, Quoits, and other sports in the grove" and a dancing platform that "terpsichorean experts" claimed to be the "best they ever shook a foot on." The oval course laid out by William Shuman in 1879 was still in use for "Racing On The Track." Admission was free, and there was a "first class refreshment stand."

The photograph on the back of this 1884 annual park pass is presumed to be that of Lucy Gay. (Courtesy Victor and Elizabeth Davidson.)

Two

Davidson's Park Becomes Riverside Park

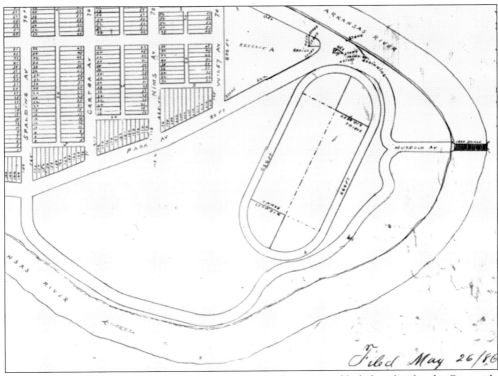

During the boom years of the late 1880s, a group of investors filed the plat for the Riverside Addition on March 26, 1886. Their intention was to establish Riverside as the premier suburban residential area of the city. In the plat, the area now known as Central Riverside Park was set aside as a reserve and not divided into house lots. Prominently depicted in that area is a half-mile oval racetrack. Also visible are scenic drives and a new bridge at Oak Street, which the investors would build as a free public bridge. (Courtesy Sedgwick County Register of Deeds.)

A principal figure in the Riverside Land Company was James Oakley Davidson (almost always referred to simply as J. O. Davidson), a prominent Wichita capitalist. He was the one always quoted in the newspaper in regard to the development of the Riverside Addition. His high visibility in association with the development led to the park in Riverside being known as Davidson's Park. (Courtesy Wichita/Sedgwick County Historical Museum.)

ONE OF THE BEAUTIFUL DRIVES IN RIVERSIDE PARK.
WICHITA, KANSAS.

As soon as it opened, the park became a popular riding destination for Wichita horse owners. Very few races were held on the racetrack oval; it was more often used for leisurely Sunday afternoon rides, such as the one this young woman appears to be taking. However, impromptu races often occurred between buggy drivers who wanted to see whose horse had the best legs.

To make the Riverside Addition a successful real estate venture, access across the river was essential. The Riverside Land Company built a bridge at the easternmost point in the area at Oak Street (now Murdock Street), which offered the most direct access to the center of town. It was not a cheap wooden bridge but a much more substantial iron truss design on concrete pilings. (Courtesy Wichita/Sedgwick County Historical Museum.)

To further enhance access to Riverside and emphasize its upscale character, J. O. Davidson and his partners incorporated the Riverside and Suburban streetcar line to provide passenger rail service to the area. The line crossed the Little River on a bridge built in 1887, one block south of Oak Street at Pine Street. The bridge became too rickety to use in 1897, and a new route for the line was established two years later.

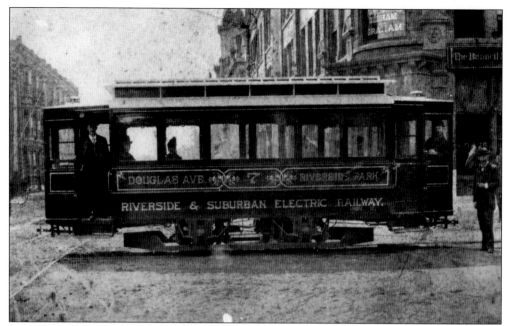

The Riverside streetcar line had fancy cars like this, seen here in 1889, that were operated by electric motors. It was one of the first electric streetcar lines in the nation. At the time, other lines in Wichita were pulled by mules or had coal-fired steam engines. In the photograph, Mrs. J. O. Davidson is visible inside on the left; the supervisor of the line, Thomas Fitch, is standing on the right.

The Riverside streetcar line carried 12,000 passengers to the park for the Fourth of July celebration in 1889—the largest single-day total for passengers on a streetcar line in Wichita up until then. Large events such as this or circus performances were a major source of income for the line. There were scarcely any residences in Riverside until after 1900, so daily commuter traffic was not significant. (Courtesy Wichita/Sedgwick County Historical Museum.)

ALONG THE CAR LINE, RIVERSIDE PARK
WICHITA, KANSAS

No. 4808

The Riverside streetcar line curved through the south part of the park after it crossed the bridge at Pine Street. The poles supporting the overhead wires were painted white and are often seen in photographs of the park from that time. After the route was abandoned in the late 1890s, the grade was used for a walking path in the park (see map on page 48).

A side-wheel steamer named *Lakeside* was bought by J. O. Davidson in 1886. It was docked at the Oak Street Bridge and could carry up to 25 people. George Parham had two naphtha-powered launches on the river in 1898. A ride from the Oak Street Bridge to the dam was 10¢. For 25¢, one could go to the dam, then up to Twelfth Street and back—over an hour-long trip. (Courtesy Wichita/Sedgwick County Historical Museum.)

Boats of all sorts were used on the Little River over the years. Some of the investors in the Riverside Land Company hailed from New England, and perhaps one of them owned this curiously designed vessel, reminiscent of the swan boats used on the lake in the Boston Common since 1877. (Courtesy Wichita/Sedgwick County Historical Museum.)

This 1888 map of Wichita shows the different names the parks had then. The new streetcar line built by the Riverside Land Company is shown crossing the Little River at Pine Street, then taking a scenic route through Davidson's Park before heading off into the residential area. The rivers join upriver from where they do presently, and it can be seen how far west the waterworks island stretched. (Courtesy Wichita State University Library, Department of Special Collections.)

This photograph shows a lone boater on the Little Arkansas River north of Davidson's (Central Riverside) Park. The view faces southeast towards the Oak Street Bridge, and the clock tower of the new county courthouse, completed in 1890, is visible above the tree line. The barbed wire fence in the foreground indicates that the land on the north side probably had livestock on it at the time this photograph was taken. (Courtesy Wichita State University Library, Department of Special Collections.)

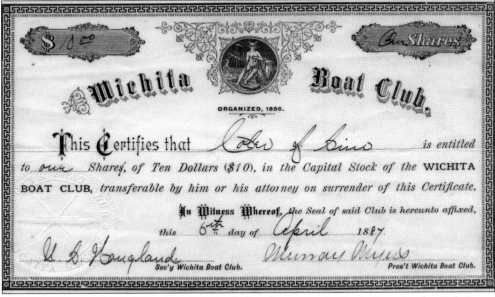

The Wichita Boat Club, formed in 1886, had a boathouse on the Little River by the Oak Street Bridge. Several of its watercraft were paper-hulled boats produced by Waters, Balch and Company of Troy, New York. One of them was big enough for six oarsmen and a coxswain. The club had 160 members at its peak, but it was disbanded by 1893 as a casualty of the economic depression. (Courtesy Greg Hissem.)

Davidson's Park was typically where circuses would set up when they came to town in the 1890s. Ringling Brothers, Barnum and Bailey, Forepaugh, Hagenbeck-Wallace, Howe and Cushing, and Sells Brothers Circuses all performed there. They would arrive by train, have a parade through downtown, and then head over to the park. Eight elephants were led across the river on July 24, 1898, as a final flourish for the arrival ceremony.

Wichita had an active community of bicyclists in the late 1800s. They often held races at the track in (South) Riverside Park and elsewhere. In 1888, they laid out a quarter-mile cinder track within the half-mile oval in Davidson's (Central Riverside) Park. A club called the Wichita Wheelmen was organized in 1896. More recently, the Riverside Parks have been where the annual Wichita River Festival Criterium bicycle races were held. (Courtesy Wichita/Sedgwick County Historical Museum.)

Three

THREE RIVERSIDE PARKS

Finlay Ross was a prosperous merchant who acted as mayor twice, from 1897 to 1900 and again in 1905 and 1906. During his first term, he orchestrated the purchase of the land that became South, Central, and North Riverside Parks. He also arranged for the donation of, or even bought outright, several key features in the new public parks, such as the Spanish cannon, the Murdock Street arch, and the *Boy With a Boot* fountain. Although the bond issue to purchase the land passed by a 3-to-1 margin, there were still opponents of public parks. Because he lived across the river from the park, naysayers derided the city's new acquisition as "Finlay Ross's backyard." The passage of time has more than justified the vision that Ross and others shared of a system of public green spaces along the rivers. (Courtesy Wichita/Sedgwick County Historical Museum.)

WICHITA HISTORICAL PANELS
BY DICK LONG AND BEN HAMMOND

Wichita Eagle cartoonist Ben Hammond and writer Dick Long created a series of historical vignettes in the early 1940s. This one depicts Finlay Ross (left) negotiating the purchase of Riverside Park with Coler Sim, the agent for the New England investors who owned the land. Ross got the land for one-tenth of its value during the boom years on the condition the city build two new bridges and make other improvements. (Courtesy *Wichita Eagle*.)

Coler Lindley Sim was a key figure in the history of the Riverside Parks. As the local representative of the Keene Syndicate, he brokered the sale of Davidson's Park to the city in 1897. Had he reported the city's offer unfavorably to the owners, the sale might not have happened. He later bought the remaining local property of the syndicate, and in 1917 he donated the land that became Sim Park. (Courtesy Greg Hissem.)

RIVERSIDE PARK, WICHITA, KANSAS.

The first bridge the city built to connect to Riverside was at the north end of Wiley Street. It was named the Greiffenstein Bridge after one of Wichita's founders, who also formerly owned the property on the north side at that point. The bridge was opened on Sunday, July 3, 1898. The two new parks it connected, Central and North Riverside, were also dedicated that day.

The first Greiffenstein Bridge only lasted 10 years. It was replaced by this iron truss bridge in 1909. The photograph was taken in 1963, just before it was demolished. The current bridge was built one block to the west, providing a more direct connection from Central Avenue on the south to Thirteenth Street on the north. Moving the bridge also helped separate vehicular traffic from the parks on both sides of the river. (Courtesy Wichita Park Department.)

The Woodman Bridge was not opened until March 5, 1899. It would have been completed sooner, but connecting a street to it from Central Avenue on the south was delayed until the city negotiated the purchase of South Riverside Park from the county. It was also a wooden wagon bridge on pilings but was slightly arched in the middle, unlike the flat Greiffenstein Bridge, and was called a "Venetian design" by the *Wichita Eagle*.

After the city assumed ownership of Riverside Park, a new streetcar route was established that went west from downtown on Central Avenue before bending north and crossing the Little River just west of the new Woodman Bridge. The line continued north, angling slightly east to Nims Street and crossing the river again, before finally ending at Eleventh Street. This photograph shows a streetcar crossing the new south bridge. (Courtesy Wichita Public Library, Local History Collection.)

The lower dam on the Little River by the *Keeper of the Plains* dates to 1894. At first, it was just a mound of soil, brush, and rocks anchored by a wood-piling core, but it was later rebuilt more substantially. Its purpose was to improve boating on the river. Beginning in 1910, the pool above served as a source of cooling water for a nearby electric power plant.

Little River Dam, Wichita, Kansas.

The dam above the Central Avenue Bridge on the Little River was built in 1910 at a cost of $25,000. It replaced one located below the bridge, which was cheaply constructed in 1898 for only $600. The first dam had a very hard life, having been blown out with dynamite during two different floods in an attempt to limit the rise of the river.

Little River Dam, Wichita, Kansas.

The higher water level above the Central Avenue dam made for much better boating conditions through the Riverside area. At first, it had a viewing platform at either end, with steel wicket gates between that allowed control over the water level behind it. Years later, the south platform and wickets were removed, the top of the dam was raised, and one large moveable gate was installed at the north end.

HOLINESS CAMP MEETING
WICHITA KANS 09

South Riverside Park was a popular choice for big camp meetings. The Kansas Holiness Association held this gathering from August 20 to 30 in 1909. A Grand Army of the Republic (GAR) encampment in September 1902 had 400 individual tents and an auditorium tent seating 3,000. Over 20,000 people attended the GAR reunion held August 16–19 in 1892. (Courtesy Wichita State University Library, Department of Special Collections.)

In December 1898, this 8,440-pound, 8-inch Civil War–era cannon and the four stacks of cannonballs were placed in North Riverside Park in an area used for GAR events. The cannon had "Ft. Pitt 1865" inscribed on it, but it was apparently never finished for use, as it did not have a firing hole. The 80 cannonballs weighed a total of 7,040 pounds, or 88 pounds each.

The cannon became the hub for all the features of North Riverside Park. The *Boy With a Boot* fountain, Lily Pond, and Park Villa were added nearby in the next few years. Of those, only Park Villa and the Lily Pond remain. One of the trees by the cannon was known as the Liberty Tree. (Courtesy Wichita Public Library, Local History Collection.)

Despite a rope barrier and a sign stating, "Keep Off of the Gun," the cannon was often a setting for photographs. And despite their weight, the cannonballs sometimes went missing. One was tossed into the river nearby in 1899 and not found until six years later. The cannon was ceremonially donated as scrap iron for the war effort on October 11, 1942, along with two smaller brass cannons. (Courtesy Kansas State Historical Society.)

In 1899, L. W. Clapp converted a natural swale along the riverbank in North Riverside Park into a scenic lagoon accented by water lilies in planter boxes. This feature suffered greatly from the floods of subsequent years, needing to be redone after each deluge. After the 1923 flood, the riverbank was moved inwards and reconstructed as a levee, wiping out the lagoon forever. (Courtesy Wichita Public Library, Local History Collection.)

Burton H. Campbell constructed this elaborate residence on the west bank overlooking the Little River at Eleventh Street and North River Boulevard in 1888. J. O. Davidson and Thomas Fitch, manager of the Riverside and Suburban Street Railway, also built large stone homes in Riverside at the same time, but after the speculative bubble burst, these three homes sat nearly alone in Riverside for many years.

This photograph was taken from the tower of Campbell Castle around 1899, looking southeast towards downtown Wichita. The scenic drive in North Riverside Park can be seen on the far bank, leading back towards the Greiffenstein Bridge. Only a few rooftops peek above the trees in the Riverside Addition to the right, the nearest of which was the home of Dr. Samuel S. Noble, a dentist. (Courtesy Wichita Public Library, Local History Collection.)

Mayor Finlay Ross received a $500 raise in 1898 and used the money to purchase this unique fountain, dedicated to "the children of Wichita." It was ordered from a dealer in New York City and installed in North Riverside Park the following spring. Contemporary newspaper accounts refer to it as the "newsboy fountain," which supports the theory the design was inspired by a beloved Italian newspaper boy who drowned. (Courtesy Kansas State Historical Society.)

The fountain was placed in North Riverside Park at the fork in the park drive in a 12-foot-wide basin. In the 1920s, the sculpture was put into storage after suffering damage from vandalism and "a wild automobile." It was repaired and used in garden shows in the 1930s, and then it made a brief reappearance in the Lily Pond by Park Villa in the 1950s before finally being discarded.

Four

THE ZOO IN RIVERSIDE PARK

An easy way for people in town to get to the zoo was to take the Riverside streetcars to the west entrance. When they arrived, they saw this welcoming entrance sign. Low stone walls made from recycled streetcar pavers flanked it on either side, with exotic tropical plants topping the pillars of the wall. The wall on the left is still there, albeit a bit shorter. So many people used the streetcars, a double line was put in to allow cars to pass without impeding each other while loading and unloading passengers. The double line of tracks merged into one as it bent east towards Nims Street. The converging rails of the two lines are visible in the foreground. (Courtesy Wichita State University Library, Department of Special Collections.)

Elaborate flower beds were part of the zoo grounds, along with the park department greenhouse, which was built in 1915 for $600. The greenhouse was moved to South Riverside Park in the 1920s. When it came time to leave and catch a streetcar home, a sign overhead beckoned, "Come Again." One of the streetcars is visible just beyond the wall. (Courtesy Wichita Park Department.)

This 1916 photograph view faces southeast from the streetcar entrance toward the zoo area. Beyond the greenhouse and flower beds are a caretaker's shed, the rectangular waterfowl pond, the alligator pit, and possibly the photographer's car. Driveways wound around through the zoo at the time. As cars became more numerous, this created problems. The park driveways were completely redone in the early 1920s to better segregate and confine automobile traffic. (Courtesy Wichita Park Department.)

SCENE IN RIVERSIDE PARK,
WICHITA KANSAS.
5725

The Riverside Park Zoo was established in the southwest corner of Central Riverside Park. A meandering walkway from the racetrack oval in the middle of the park led to the zoo. Several of the freestanding pens and some old field cannons may be seen back among the trees in this view. The cannons do not appear in photographs after 1916.

RIVERSIDE PARK ZOO, WICHITA, KANS.

Whitetail deer were the first animals kept at the zoo. They were put on exhibit in July 1901. Deer were exterminated in Kansas by market and subsistence hunting in the late 1800s, as were elk, bison, and pronghorn. Deer are very common in Kansas now, but they were so scarce prior to World War II that merely seeing one would merit an item in local newspapers.

The first elk at the Central Riverside Park Zoo were three cows bought from local showman Charles Payne in November 1901; a bull was obtained the following year. As the herd increased, surplus animals were sold or traded. The sale of one elk in 1909 garnered $75, which was used to purchase the first two bears kept at the zoo. (Courtesy Wichita/Sedgwick County Historical Museum.)

From 1910 until 1918, the elk paddock was on the northern part of the zoo grounds, along with the enclosures of the bison and deer. The two-story home at 803 Wiley Street and other buildings visible in the background illustrate just how close the nearest residences were. All the neighboring structures seen here are still present.

The first bison at the zoo was obtained through a public subscription effort organized by a local newspaper, the *Wichita Beacon*. It arrived on Sunday, June 19, 1910, and was named Beacon, as is noted on the sign. Bison were quite scarce at this time, having been almost driven to extinction in the late 1800s. For a small zoo, having them on display was a notable accomplishment. (Courtesy Wichita/Sedgwick County Historical Museum.)

Beacon's tenure at the zoo was only three years. He became "cross and potentially dangerous" and was shot on December 12, 1913, before 500 onlookers. He weighed 2,030 pounds. He was butchered at the local Dold Packing Company, and the meat was sold at two downtown markets as special selections for Christmas dinners. The proceeds from the sale of his meat were used to support the zoo. (Courtesy Wichita State University Library, Department of Special Collections.)

BUFFALO IN RIVERSIDE PARK ZOO WICHITA, KANS. 5738

The deer and other hoof stock in the zoo were moved to Linwood Park in 1918 in response to complaints from the nearby residents about the "barnyard smells," especially in summer. Linwood Park is in the southeast part of town and is surrounded by homes today, but in 1918 there were few neighboring residences. In 1931, the three remaining bison were sold to the 101 Ranch near Pawhuska, Oklahoma.

BEARS IN RIVERSIDE PARK ZOO WICHITA KANS

These two bears were bought in Okeene, Oklahoma, in 1909. The small cage seen here was all the bears had to live in until a larger enclosure was built in 1922. The curved, pointed overhanging bars were a common design element of both facilities. Black bears naturally have different fur colors, and these bears were the black and light brown (cinnamon) versions.

A rectangular waterfowl pond, 33 feet by 64 feet, was constructed in July 1910. It was removed in 2003 during the recent round of park renovations. This view looks east and shows several of the small, freestanding enclosures of the time, as well as the pioneer cabin that stood in the park from 1910 to 1918. Pearl J. Conklin, who lived just across the river to the east, donated the cabin.

A white pelican was one of the first waterfowl to occupy the new pond. Pelicans were often residents there over the years. The misadventures Charles Goodrum and his father, Bernie, experienced in the acquisition of one pelican in the summer of 1938 is humorously recounted in the first chapter of Charles's 1967 book, *I'll Trade You an Elk*. This photograph looks south, and the ostrich pen is visible in the background. (Courtesy Wichita State University Library, Department of Special Collections.)

The newly formed Kansas Gas and Electric Company donated these ostriches to the Central Riverside Park Zoo. They were purchased in Phoenix and debuted in Wichita on Sunday, August 13, 1910. An estimated 10,000 people came to the park that day. The ostrich pen was located near where the Kansas Wildlife Exhibit is now. The view faces northeast, and the pioneer cabin is visible in the background.

This distinctive structure was built in 1912 on the site where the Kansas Wildlife Exhibit is today. The Park Zoo was a much more formal and substantial facility than had been built previously. It allowed several animals to be housed under one roof and demonstrates a much greater support for the zoo from the city administration. The walls were paver stones that had been removed from the downtown streetcar lines in 1911. (Courtesy Wichita Park Department.)

Park staff worked hard to have interesting gardens in the new parks. This topiary, which spells out the name of the park, was located at the northwest curve of the racetrack oval, where it was joined by the drive from the Greiffenstein Bridge. The nearly treeless area beyond this feature in the middle of the oval was where the circuses of the 1890s set up their big tents. (Courtesy Wichita Park Department.)

Visitors entering Central Riverside Park from the east over the Murdock Bridge would see these picket posts demarking the pedestrian crosswalk in the racetrack oval. Just beyond the pickets were the Spanish cannon and some of the formal garden beds. Several of the arborvitae seen here are still present. Both hoof prints and tire tracks are visible in the unpaved road in this 1916 photograph. (Courtesy Wichita Park Department.)

The Little Arkansas River, Riverside Park, Wichita, Kans.

The center section of the Woodman Bridge collapsed on June 16, 1913, due to rotten pilings. This image documents how it appeared afterward—an odd photographic choice for a postcard. It is also curious that there is no mention of the bridge's obvious disability. The photographer was upstream on the south bank of the Little River, facing west. A bit of the streetcar bridge may be seen through the gap, and one of the white poles that supported the overhead electric lines is visible to the right of the gap. The weekend following the collapse, hundreds crowded across that streetcar bridge to get to the park. During the Fourth of July celebration, R. C. Israel of the Riverside Boat House offered ferry rides to carry people across the river. It took two years for the city to replace the bridge. In an election to approve issuing $15,000 in bonds to replace the bridge, 42 percent of the 5,254 who turned out voted against it. A concrete replacement was finally built in 1915, which lasted for 60 years. (Courtesy Wichita/Sedgwick County Historical Museum.)

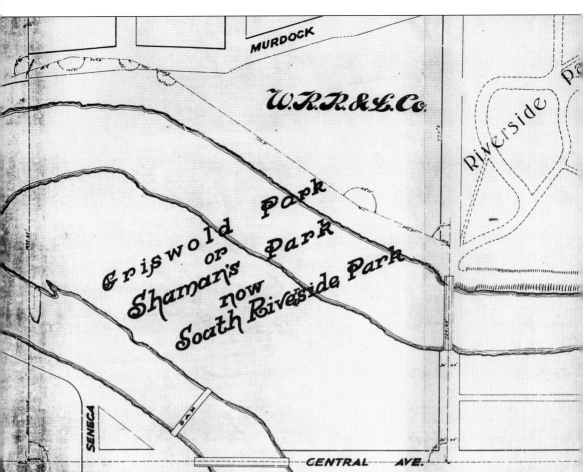

This map, dated April 1916, was produced by the city at a time when it was at odds with the streetcar company, which was in arrears for its annual franchise fees. Ultimately, in partial settlement of its obligation, the company deeded over to the city the triangular parcel of land to the west of Nims Street. It is labeled here as "W.R.R.&L.Co.," meaning Wichita Railroad and Light Company. This land was never part of the deal Mayor Finlay Ross made in 1897 when the Riverside Parks were purchased. The Riverside Land Company and the streetcar line it established were basically the same entity financially, and the title for this bit of land ended up with the streetcar line. The line, like all the other lines from that time, eventually merged into the Wichita Railroad and Light Company. After the city took possession of the land, it was suggested it be called West Riverside Park, but that idea never took root. (Courtesy City of Wichita Public Works.)

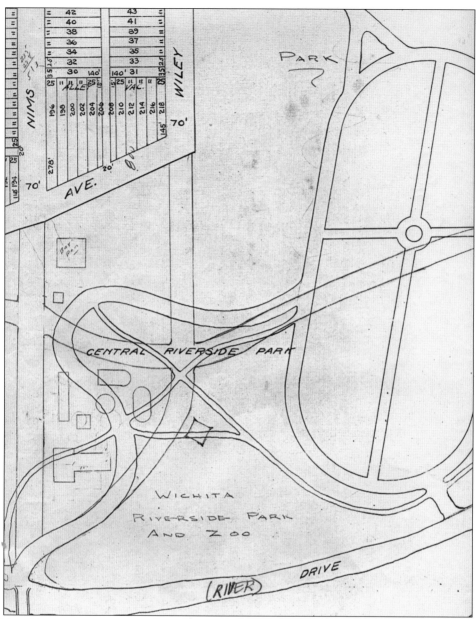

This palimpsest map was part of an old quarter-section atlas of Sedgwick County owned by the local electric utility. It lays out the drives and walking paths in the Central Riverside Park of 1898, overlaid with those that replaced them in 1921. L. W. Clapp eliminated the tangle of drives in the zoo area by establishing a simple "X" traffic pattern. One east-west drive connected to the Murdock Bridge, while one north-south drive, formed by an extension of Wiley Street, connected the Woodman Bridge on the south with the Greiffenstein Bridge to the north. It also illustrates where the zoo buildings were relative to those drives and paths. The narrow path that curves down below the racetrack oval and angles up toward Nims Avenue was originally the grade of J. O. Davidson's streetcar line built in 1887. When the Greiffenstein Bridge was moved west to Nims Avenue in 1963, Wiley ceased to be a through street. The extension of Wiley Street through the park was removed in the 1980s.

Bear Mountain, built in 1922, was much larger than the old enclosure for the bears; it had small caves for birthing and sleeping. When the bears were first introduced to their new home, two cubs found a place where the iron bars were not properly fastened and escaped. They were recaptured shortly afterwards without incident, and the missing bolts were installed. (Courtesy Wichita Park Department.)

A "tropical house" was also built a short distance to the east of the Bear Mountain in 1922. It housed tropical plants and exotic birds, but it only lasted for 20 years. Its demise can be easily imagined by considering the cumulative effect of the condensation that must have drained off all the windows onto the wood framework. Coal-burning, pot-bellied stoves were brought in to supply additional heat in winter. (Courtesy Wichita Public Library, Local History Collection.)

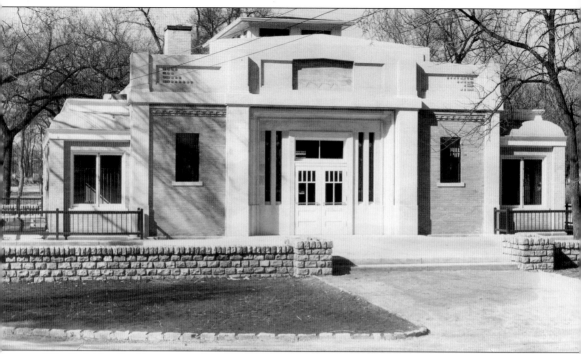

The Park Zoo Building was replaced with an upgraded version in 1927. It was constructed on the same site where the Park Zoo had originally stood. It shared many features with its predecessor, such as double-door entries on either end, a clerestory for ventilation and light, and cages for the animals on both sides, which had inside and outside viewing opportunities for the public. A special room in the basement was reserved as winter quarters for the alligators. The paver stones from the Park Zoo Building were used to make a low rock wall around the site. (Courtesy Wichita Park Department.)

The big cats were kept on the south side of the building. The male lion seen here was named King. The new building had a secluded room in the basement for when the lioness was ready to give birth. That was not only a more humane way to keep them in captivity, but it also made for successful rearing of lion cubs, a valuable source of income for the zoo. (Courtesy Wichita Park Department.)

The north side of the building was where the monkeys were kept. Some cages held only one species of primate; sometimes different species might be housed together if they were able to get along with each other. In later years, small freestanding cages were added to the public space in the middle of the building for animals such as iguanas and snakes. (Courtesy Wichita Park Department.)

The oval waterfowl pond seen here was built in 1913. The circular alligator pit is also visible as it was first built, without any fencing over the top. Until a fenced top was added, zoo lore says some mean-spirited park goers tossed ducks in. The Pagoda Building, a restroom at the time, is partially visible on the left in this 1926 photograph. (Courtesy Wichita Park Department.)

Chico, a female brown capuchin monkey, was donated to the zoo in 1930. She made this star appearance in a special photogravure section of the *Wichita Eagle* on Sunday, May 31, 1931, along with keeper Claude White. Also featured on the page titled, "Among the Denizens of the Zoo," was King the lion, a bear, a leopard, a sandhill crane, and a trio of rhesus monkeys. (Courtesy *Wichita Eagle*.)

I'll Trade You an Elk
Charles A. Goodrum

During the depths of the Depression, a schoolteacher named Bernie Goodrum was hired by the Wichita Park Department to head its recreation program, which included the zoo. Thirty years later, his son wrote a very entertaining memoir of those years titled *I'll Trade You an Elk*. The book was released in 1967, just as public interest was building in Wichita to develop a new, larger zoo. The book served as inspiration for two episodes of the *Wonderful World of Disney* television show in 1970, with Hal Holbrook playing the father character in the *Wacky Zoo of Morgan City*. (Courtesy Seymour Chwast.)

The longest-tenured residents of the Central Riverside Park Zoo were three American alligators named Grandpa, One-Eye, and Lady. Zoo records show they lived there from 1910 to 1972. Moving them in the spring from their winter home beneath the Lion House to their summer home in the alligator pit and then back inside again in the fall were much-anticipated annual events. (Courtesy Wichita Park Department.)

When it was time to move the alligators to their summer home, the heat was shut off to the basement holding room to make the animals more lethargic, thus easier to move. Still, it was never a simple thing to do. This photograph was taken during the spring move for Grandpa on May 12, 1961, as he was eased out of the holding room. (Courtesy Wichita Park Department.)

A two-wheel
trailer ordinarily
used for moving
telephone poles
and root-balled
trees was enlisted
to transport the
alligators across
the zoo grounds. It
took four people:
one to pull and
clear the way, one
to push, one to
steady the animal,
and one to hold
the tail. The zoo
staff always moved
the alligators late
in the day on a
Friday to promote
public attendance.
(Courtesy Wichita
Park Department.)

The procession
from the zoo
building to the
alligator pit was
quite a parade,
as children took
special delight
in joining in.
Needless to
say, this was a
simpler time.
Zoos nowadays
are not likely to
promote public
involvement in
routine chores,
especially those
involving large,
toothy reptiles.
(Courtesy Wichita
Park Department.)

At the alligator pit, the trailer was backed up to the doorway, and the animal was carefully lowered in. After all the alligators were moved, the water was turned on to fill the display, and the alligator's summer routine would begin: basking in the sun all day and, once in awhile, actually moving around. They were fed on Sunday afternoon at 3:00 p.m. (Courtesy Wichita Park Department.)

With the transfer ritual completed, the crowd watches to see what the alligators will do next. Thousands of people observed the moving of the alligators over the span of six decades, and an article on the subject usually appeared in the newspaper the following day. The alligators were sent to the Mohawk Zoo in Tulsa in 1972, where they spent their final years. (Courtesy Wichita Park Department.)

Five

HISTORIC FEATURES IN THE RIVERSIDE PARKS

Reuben Carl "R. C." Israel established the Riverside Boat House around 1905 and owned it until his death in 1924. He was a successful local realtor and entrepreneur. The Israel residence was a block north of the Murdock Bridge at 911 North Waco Street. The Boat House was a family business, and R. C.'s wife, Julia Ann, ran it from 1924 until 1938. Their daughter Celia and her husband, Basil Carter, ran it until 1954. (Courtesy family of Noble and Eleanor Carter.)

The first Riverside Boat House was a small, pagoda-like playhouse R. C. had originally built for his children in his backyard. It is visible here to the left of the man in the dark suit. Structures were added or rebuilt over the next several years, both at the street and river level, so the Boat House appears slightly different in the various photographs taken before 1920. (Courtesy family of Noble and Eleanor Carter.)

The first name of the business was the Murdock Avenue Boat House, visible in the sign over the porch of the building seen here, which faces north. The Boat House began informally in the summer of 1898, when R. C. provided his two sons, Robert and Carl, with six rowboats to rent to the public as a way to keep them busy. The boats were merely kept tied up under the bridge. (Courtesy family of Noble and Eleanor Carter.)

R. C. Israel acquired this motor launch in 1911. He named it the *Bessie Mae* after one of his daughters. It was used to carry small groups on tours up and down the river. The fare was 10¢ per passenger. It was also used for retrieving unreturned rowboats and canoes at the end of the day. (Courtesy family of Noble and Eleanor Carter.)

High dives from a platform atop the boat House were popular entertainment at special events. Various daredevils made this performance over the years, with the longest-tenured diver being Harold "Buddy" Siegel, from 1922 to 1935. The river was naturally deeper at this point, but dredging by the city during the 1910s and 1920s made it even deeper, and thus safer for the divers. (Courtesy family of Noble and Eleanor Carter.)

The Riverside Boat House was rebuilt in its final form in 1920, with high-columned facades facing Murdock Street and the river. Over the next three decades, it continued to be a vital part of the recreational and social scene of Wichita. Boating on the river waned in popularity after World War II, and the Boat House went into decline. It was razed during January 1968 in an urban renewal project.

The 1886 iron bridge was replaced with a concrete structure in 1925. It featured viewing platforms on each side, as well as stairways leading down to the river at both ends of the bridge, which was indicative of how much activity was at the Riverside Boat House then. The deck was replaced in 2005, but the sidewalks and platforms were left unchanged, and the bridge still looks now much like it did in 1925. (Courtesy Wichita State University Library, Department of Special Collections.)

The boat in this 1940 photograph, named *Mischief*, was the last motor launch used at the Riverside Boat House. Celia, the daughter of R. C. and Julia Ann, is on the dock with her husband, Basil Carter. Their son Clayton is driving, with his cousin Julia Ann Israel beside him. In the front seat are Elizabeth, R. C.'s sister, and her husband, Jake Hollinger. Mickey the terrier was always happy to take a ride on the river. (Courtesy Family of Noble and Eleanor Carter.)

Gene Mason, the author's father, moved to Wichita from Des Moines in 1939 to work in the aircraft plants. For Memorial Day weekend, he invited down Bee Tham, a young woman he was courting from back home, and told her to bring along his sister and mother. That Sunday, the four enjoyed a picnic in Central Riverside Park. Gene proposed to Bee that day on a canoe ride, and she accepted.

This double arch was built at the north entry to Central Riverside Park in 1900, just south of the Greiffenstein Bridge. People used both horse-powered transportation and streetcars to reach the parks. Few streets outside of downtown were paved, but this would change rapidly over the next two decades, due in no small part to the advent of the automobile. The first automobile arrived in Wichita on December 23, 1899. The sign seen here (to the right) forbids passage of any heavy vehicles through the park. Violators of the posted rules were subject to a minimum of a $5 fine and up to a maximum of $50, a considerable sum at the time. The parks were supposed to be places of enjoyment for everyone, and visitors were expected to behave in a manner respectful of other people, as well as the park itself and all it contained. (Courtesy Wichita State University Library, Department of Special Collections.)

Mayor Finlay Ross arranged for this distinctive feature at the Murdock Street entrance to Central Riverside Park. It was moved there in late 1900, but it did not receive the veneer of brick and the metal cornice on top until a year later. A park regulations sign is visible through the left pedestrian arch. The Riverside Boat House was located on the south side of the street at this point. (Courtesy family of Noble and Eleanor Carter.)

The Riverside Arch was formerly used for a grand entryway to the downtown street fairs in autumn of 1899 and 1900. The fairs were held on South Main and Market Streets and featured a wide variety of amusements. The triple-looped arches seen here were retained to function as the east gateway to the park, except the smaller side arches were opened up for pedestrian use. (Courtesy Wichita/Sedgwick County Historical Museum.)

A fall street fair and carnival was held in downtown Wichita for several years beginning in 1899. These buttons were sold for 10¢ in association with the 1899 and 1900 fairs. At least three different button designs are known from each year. The street fairs and the use of a button to identify attendees served as a model for the Wichita River Festival, which has been held in late spring every year since it began in 1973. (Both courtesy Wichita/Sedgwick County Historical Museum.)

The Riverside Arch spanned the Murdock Street park entrance for only 12 years. An inspection by the fire marshal in January 1913 determined the arch was a public safety hazard. Its wooden framework had settled and shifted out of line, causing cracks in the brick veneer. In addition, its roof had been damaged by a fire at the adjacent Riverside Boat House that winter. The arch was removed in March 1913. (Courtesy Family of Noble and Eleanor Carter.)

The bandstand shown here was built on the north end of Central Riverside Park in 1899. An article in the April 16, 1899, *Wichita Eagle* describes "an elegant band stand" to be constructed about 200 yards from the Greiffenstein Bridge, octagonal in shape and seating a 20-piece band. "The platform will be five feet high, and from there 12 feet to the top of the circular roof." (Courtesy Wichita/Sedgwick County Historical Museum.)

In its early years, the park was a botanical showcase. In 1900, park gardener George E. Harris sculpted some of the evergreen trees into topiaries. One of these took the form of a hen sitting on a nest. Across the walk, another topiary looked like an egg in a nest. He also created elaborate display beds, one of which was located near the *Boy With a Boot* fountain and featured gold and green *Alternantheras*, spelling the words "au revoir." Disastrous floods occurred in the summers

of both 1903 and 1904, wiping out all the elaborate flower beds the city had worked so hard to create, as well as the carefully built-up and graded park drives. The 1904 flood was the second-worst recorded flood in Wichita, exceeded only by the 1877 flood. (Courtesy Kansas State Historical Society.)

Thousands of people would sometimes visit Riverside Park on holidays or weekends. Some would have picnics, like these three young people seated near the bandstand. Others would cruise the park drives in their buggies, listen to concerts, stroll the grounds to look at the flower beds, or just relax in the shade on one of the many benches. (Courtesy Wichita State University Library, Department of Special Collections.)

The Pagoda Building was constructed in 1911 as a concession stand. Designed by William R. Stringfield, it illustrates the strong Japanese influence of the time. It was remodeled for use as a public restroom from 1913 to 1938. The women's room was on the north side, the men's was on the southeast, and the remainder of the interior was a waiting room. It has been used for storage in recent years.

The granite fountain located in Victoria Park at Seventeenth Street and Park Place was originally donated to the city in November 1910 by the National Humane Alliance as a place for animals to enjoy a drink of water. The large upper basin was for horses, and the smaller bowls below were for dogs. It was placed downtown in the middle of the intersection of St. Francis and William Streets.

The fountain was soon seen as impractical in the downtown location, but efforts to move it proved controversial. When that intersection was repaved in August 1919, the city seized the opportunity to move the fountain, and it was taken to Central Riverside Park. It sat across the street to the north of the rectangular waterfowl pond and is barely visible on the right edge of this 1949 photograph. It was moved to its present location in 1977. (Courtesy Wichita Park Department.)

The old cannon located in Central Riverside Park in the triangle west of Nims Street was captured in Cuba during the Spanish-American War in 1898. It weighs 800 pounds and was cast in Seville, Spain, in 1794. Mayor Finlay Ross obtained the cannon for Wichita in 1900. Together with the *Hiker* statue, it forms Wichita's Spanish-American War Memorial.

The cannon was originally located near the middle of the park at the east end of the crosswalk in the racetrack oval. It faced traffic entering the park from the Murdock Bridge (see page 45). The cannon was placed in its present location on the triangle of land west of Nims Street when the *Hiker* statue was donated to the city in 1926.

Lawton Post No. 18 of the United Spanish War Veterans gave the *Hiker* to the city in 1926. The statue was created by Allen G. Newman in 1904 and cast at the Williams Foundry in New York City in 1926. Copies of this statue were placed in many cities nationwide in the early 1900s. Both 7- and 9-foot-tall versions were made; Wichita's is 7 feet tall.

This rustic stage was constructed with federal public works funds a short distance west of Nims Street in Central Riverside Park in the 1930s. It replaced a bandstand built in 1918 that formerly stood a short distance to the southwest, close to where the last public swimming hole was located. Ranks of wooden benches on concrete supports once faced the stage. Behind the benches was an elevated projection booth for showing outdoor movies.

Due to complaints about rough streets from the increasing number of motorists, in 1911 the city ordered the removal of the Colorado sandstone pavers around the streetcar tracks downtown. The pavers provided traction for the mules that originally pulled the streetcars, and the city inherited over 5,000 square yards of them. They were used for constructing various features, like these in Central Riverside Park, and for edging sidewalks and driveways.

This building, constructed in 1921 and designed by L. W. Clapp, currently houses the office and workrooms for the Kansas Wildlife Exhibit. The west part was originally a picnic shelter, and the zoo office was in the east part. Through the now-closed arched doorway was a concession stand. The west part was rebuilt as restrooms in 1938, taking over that function from the Pagoda Building.

Six

THE OTHER
RIVERSIDE PARKS

Entrance to Wonderland Park, Wichita, Kans.

Wonderland Park was a private amusement park located on Ackerman's Island north of the Second Street Bridge. It was partially complete in the fall of 1905, but had its grand opening on Saturday, April 28, 1906. Around 12,000 people enjoyed the park on the Fourth of July that year, and it continued to be a favorite recreation spot for over a decade. The highest daily attendance was on July 4, 1915, when it received over 19,000 patrons.

Between 1870 and 1900, a large island formed in the Arkansas River, stretching from Douglas Avenue north to the confluence with the Little Arkansas. The island formed in part due to ditch irrigation companies in western Kansas drawing off much of the water in the river for agriculture. In 1887, Joseph Ackerman purchased a tract of real estate that encompassed the island, which came to bear his name. (Courtesy the Sanborn Library LLC.)

The third Douglas Avenue Bridge was a concrete version built in 1909. It had seven spans originally, but only five now, as the river was much wider then. Visible above the far (north) railing is a large electric sign advertising Wonderland Park, an amusement park on Ackerman's Island in the river. This sign was visible after dark for over a mile to the east along Douglas Avenue.

This theater was one of the attractions at Wonderland Park during its early years. The stage hosted vaudeville acts, and the theater could seat approximately 800 on the main floor and 300 in the balcony. It was located at the north end of the island, near the roller coaster. The building was remodeled and housed a natatorium (indoor pool) after 1911, which remained in use until the park closed in 1917. (Courtesy Wichita/Sedgwick County Historical Museum.)

When the first theater building was remodeled, stage productions were still offered in a pavilion near the south entrance gate. In June 1913, the bill for one week included the Alpha Sextette singers, the Darting Darts (acrobats), xylophonist Lew Fitzgibbons, Beck and Henney (piano, song, and dance), and C. C. Burnison and K. Taylor performing their two-scene play *Graham's Valet*. Three shows were offered daily. (Courtesy Wichita State University Library, Department of Special Collections.)

Four statues were centrally located on the grounds of Wonderland Park in a diamond-shaped arrangement. They were salvaged from the St. Louis World's Fair of 1904. They arrived in damaged condition on January 17, 1906, were restored as well as possible, and put on display. They only lasted another four years, as they were made of staff (a mixture of plaster and hemp) and did not hold up well to external conditions.

Popular tunes rendered by local ensembles enlivened the air at Wonderland Park. Frederick H. Innes and his Orchestral Band played on the first opening day, April 28, 1906. The park band would sometimes hop on a streetcar and travel around town playing music as a way to promote Wonderland Park, as well as provide a pleasant amusement for the public.

The roller coaster was a popular feature at Wonderland Park. It was located on the north side of the island next to the dance pavilion. At first, it was in the relatively simple figure-eight configuration seen here. Wonderland Park closed in 1917, due largely to the passage of the blue laws that forbade charging admission on Sundays. The park grounds were used by the Arkansas Valley Interurban Railway from 1920 to 1933.

One of the changes to Wonderland Park done in 1911 was to greatly expand the roller coaster, making in one of the largest in the United States. The new ride was called the Giant Thriller. This photograph looks south toward Ackerman's Island from the east bank of the Arkansas River, just below the junction with the Little River. (Courtesy Wichita Public Library, Local History Collection.)

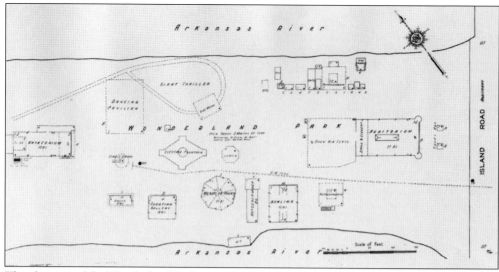

This drawing of the Wonderland Park grounds was part of the 1914 Sanborn Fire Insurance maps of Wichita. Shown are the natatorium, dance pavilion, roller coaster, shooting gallery, merry-go-round, bowling alley, open-air theater, and a *katzenjammer* (fun house). A less glamorous, but essential feature is shown at the lower center: the "w. c.," or water closet, was unfortunately located directly on the bank of the river. (Courtesy the Sanborn Library LLC.)

The Wichita Baseball and Athletic Association formed in 1912 to raise the cash for construction of a baseball stadium on Ackerman's Island between Second Street and Douglas Avenue. It was known as Island Park. The hometown semi-pro team played here until 1933, when the facility was torn down and Lawrence Stadium was built a half mile south. (Courtesy Greg Hissem.)

This is how Ackerman's Island appeared from August 1920 through 1933, as seen from the top of the Broadview Hotel. The north-facing grandstand of Island Park baseball stadium is just beyond the two railroad bridges, and the shops and car barns of the Arkansas Valley Interurban Railroad occupy the north part of the island where Wonderland Park once stood. (Courtesy Wichita Public Library, Local History Section.)

An exhibition match between the Wichita Jobbers and the Chicago White Sox on Thursday, April 4, 1912, was the first game played at Island Park. Football games were played here in the offseason, both at the high school and collegiate level, with the crosstown rivalry between Friends University and Wichita University always being hotly contested. (Courtesy Wichita/Sedgwick County Historical Museum.)

On the evening of Thursday, October 7, 1915, a balloon race began at Island Park. Four balloons were inflated with natural gas and took off, drifting toward the southeast. The newly formed Wichita Aero Club had two entries, *Wichita I* and *Wichita II*. The winner of the race was the *St. Louis*, which came down 13 hours later near Prescott, Arkansas, after reaching an altitude of 13,000 feet and traveling 363 miles. (Courtesy Wichita/Sedgwick County Historical Museum.)

Delos P. Woods, president of the Wichita Aero Club, took this photograph of Ackerman's Island as his balloon, *Wichita II*, ascended over downtown. This is the first aerial photograph of Wichita. The balloon race received national attention, and in the following decades airplane manufacturing developed into a major industry in Wichita. Beech, Cessna, and Stearman (Boeing) all began and remain in Wichita, the "Air Capital of the World." (Courtesy Wichita/Sedgwick County Historical Museum.)

Hundreds of men working with shovels and wheelbarrows dug up the east side of Ackerman's Island and dumped it into the former west channel of the river during the winter of 1933–1934. The river had ceased to flow through the west channel by then, except during a flood. This Civil Works Administration project resulted in the river channel as it is today. (Courtesy Wichita/ Sedgwick County Historical Museum.)

This is how the river looked once the project was finished. McLean Boulevard would eventually be built along the new west bank, as well as new shops for the Arkansas Valley Interurban to replace what was formerly on Ackerman's Island. These two photographs, taken from atop the Broadview Hotel, were included in the 1934 annual report of the Works Progress Administration (WPA) as documentation of the prior year's accomplishments. (Courtesy Wichita Public Library, Local History Collection.)

Exploration Place, Wichita's science museum, opened in April 2000. It sits on the same spot where Wonderland Park was, on the west bank of the Arkansas River north of the Second Street Bridge. The dramatic design of the building was created by world-renowned architect Moshe Safde. Inside are 100,000 square feet of permanent and traveling exhibits, a café, and one of the only CyberDome interactive theaters in the world.

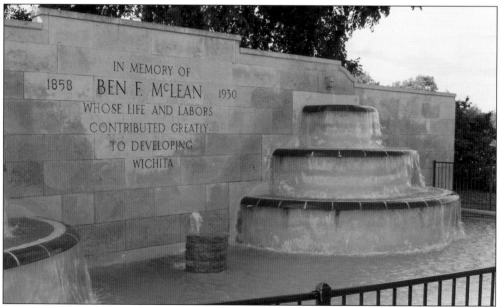

The McLean Memorial Fountain was built in 1935 on the west bank of the Arkansas River just north of Douglas. It honors Ben F. McLean, who served Wichita between 1894 and 1924 as mayor, city councilman, and park commissioner. The boulevard that runs along the west side of the river is also named for him, as was the bridge at Seneca Street. He formerly lived at 313 North Seneca Street.

Following the removal of Island Park, the Civil Works Administration constructed a new baseball stadium in 1934. It was located a half mile south on the west bank of the Arkansas River in a field once known as Payne's pasture. It was named for Robert Lawrence, a prominent west side citizen during Wichita's early years. It was extensively remodeled in 1972 and renamed Lawrence-Dumont Stadium.

The long history of baseball in Wichita is celebrated in the National Baseball Congress Walk of Fame, a special display along the outfield fence added in 2002. In 1935, Hap Dumont kicked off the first National Baseball Congress tournament by offering Satchel Paige $1,000 to bring his racially integrated team from Bismarck, North Dakota. Satchel struck out 60 batters and won four games, a tournament record that still stands.

Lewis W. Clapp was president of the Wichita Park Board from its inception in 1920 until his death in 1934. He had previously served as city commissioner, mayor, and city manager. He was always a strong advocate for the parks and initiated the formation of the Wichita Park Board. Clapp did the landscape design for Oak, Sim, and the Riverside Parks, as well as the architectural design of several park structures. (Courtesy Wichita/Sedgwick County Historical Museum.)

Arthur B. Sim Memorial Park was donated to Wichita in 1917 by Coler Sim in memory of his son. It covers 181 acres of land a mile west of downtown on the east bank of the Arkansas River. The park includes an 18-hole golf course and a picnic area set in the sand hills along the river. The monumental entryway was designed by L. W. Clapp.

In 1943, the Munger House was purchased by the Eunice Sterling chapter of the Daughters of the American Revolution and given to Historic Wichita, Inc., in 1952. It became one of four founding structures in the Old Cowtown Museum, which is on the north bank of the Arkansas River west of downtown. Old Cowtown is a living museum that recreates life in Wichita prior to 1880.

The Old Cowtown Museum began on 25 acres of land owned by the Wichita Water Company, which was accepted by the City of Wichita on a 99-year lease in 1951. Historic buildings from Wichita's earliest days have been relocated here, restored, and now line the streets. Reenactors in period dress greet visitors and explain the historical significance of the buildings. A working 1870s farm is also part of the museum.

Members of a local whist club, which included former Kansas governor William Stanley, incorporated the Riverside Club Association in December 1908. They bought some land at the northwest corner of Briggs Street and North River Boulevard, right across the Little River from North Riverside Park. The Riverside Club House opened February 24, 1910, next door to the Campbell Castle. The streetcar line was extended north on Porter Street to reach it. (Courtesy Greg Hissem.)

The facility was rented for meetings and social events. It had boats, a two-lane bowling alley, tennis courts, and a swimming beach. The Riverside Club foundered in 1917, and the property was repossessed. It was bought by the Midian Shrine, which used it until 1927. It next went to the school board, who scrapped the building but did nothing with the land. Gloria Dei Lutheran Church now occupies the site.

Municipal Bathing Beach,
Wichita, Kansas

A public swimming hole was opened on Friday, August 11, 1911, in South Riverside Park at the first bend of the Little River above the Central Avenue dam, directly across from where the Art Museum is today. It was called the Municipal Beach. Swimming trunks were available for rent, and those with their own trunks could swim for free. The city improved the river for this new attraction by dredging it deeper and creating a sandy "beach," hence the name. In 1915, the Municipal Beach moved a short distance upstream to the north bank of the Little River, about 100 yards west of the Woodman Bridge. It was completed just as the Woodman Bridge was rebuilt, taking advantage of the lower water level in the river to install the piers in the riverbed. It had a 200-foot-long bathhouse with changing rooms for 48 women and 82 men.

In 1923, the public swimming hole in the Little River was done away with when a large concrete swimming pool was built in South Riverside Park, located where the tennis center is today. The pool was 275 feet long by 235 feet wide, with an irregular round shape. It had a 60-foot-wide sandy area

on the north side and retained the name Municipal Beach. Nearly 115,000 people used the pool during the summer of 1929. About the same time, the greenhouse from the zoo area was relocated to this park. It sat just to the southwest of the pool. (Courtesy Wichita Park Department.)

In 1938, the Municipal Beach was rebuilt by WPA labor in a 240-foot-by-125-foot rectangular shape with two small kiddie pools at the north end. It also had 38 thousand-watt underwater lights for illuminating the pool in the evening. During the Depression, annual pool patronage dropped off, but it increased to 104,000 by 1951. (Courtesy Wichita State University Library, Department of Special Collections.)

The pool varied from 2 to 9 feet deep. Two water slides were a favorite attraction; the taller one shown, with the hump in the middle, was for the more daring. In 1969, continued operation of the pool was deemed impractical, and it was closed. The Ralph Wulz Riverside Tennis Center now occupies the site. Eleven smaller public pools still serve the citizens of Wichita in parks across the city.

Junction of the "Little" and "Big" Arkansas Rivers, Wichita, Kansas

SK5474

This aerial view from around 1939 shows the Municipal Beach in its final configuration. Across the river to the south, where the Indian Center is today, were the park shops and a big hill of sand and silt dredged from the river in 1925. On its west slope facing Seneca Street, park staff would plant a garden in the shape of a large "W" every year. In snowy winters, this same hill was used for sledding. The hill was cut down and reshaped when the Mid-America All-Indian Center was built in 1975. In 1935, all streetcar service in Wichita ended, and the Riverside streetcar line bridge next to the Woodman Bridge was removed. Visible in the lower right corner is the first building of the Wichita Art Museum, erected in 1935. (Courtesy Wichita/Sedgwick County Historical Museum.)

The Wichita Art Museum is located on the west bank of the Little River, just across from South Riverside Park. It was begun with a bequest from Louise Caldwell Murdock, who died in 1915 and was the widow of Roland P. Murdock, co-owner of the *Wichita Eagle*. The museum is nationally recognized for its collection of 20th-century American art, and its total holdings amount to over 7,000 works of art. The small building it began with in 1935 was added to in 1963 before being totally redone in the 1970s and expanded in 2003. The new grand entry hall has a large Dale Chihuly blown-glass sculpture hanging from the ceiling. The museum's 75th anniversary was in 2010.

This small pool was just west of Nims Street in South Riverside Park. It was used for a waterfowl display and a children's wading pool between 1900 and 1915. James R. Mead, in a July 5, 1900, letter to the *Wichita Eagle*, stated that this feature predated the town. There has been no water in it for decades, but a circular depression can still be seen at the site. The railing of the Woodman Bridge is visible in the background. (Courtesy Wichita Public Library, Local History Section.)

The Lily Pond in North Riverside Park was built in 1902. The pond has held goldfish and various other fish over the years, as well as planter boxes of aquatic lilies. It owes it shape to having been built along a preexisting curved depression, which was probably a spot where clay was excavated for the Brunswick Stone Company, a brickworks located nearby in the late 1880s.

View in Riverside Park, Wichita, Kansas.

In 1907, a local photographer named Jesse Todd created a scandal when he sought to take a picture of a mermaid in the Lily Pond. After a complaint from an offended passerby about public nudity, Todd was arrested and fined $25. This fanciful postcard based on the notorious episode appeared the following year. On the back is this poem written by the model, known only as "Mona."

THE MERMAID'S SOLILOQUY

They say I am a naughty girl,
The worst in Wichita;
For the way I had my picture made;
It was against the law.
Now that good book don't say,
In Matthew, Mark, Luke or John,
That when you have a picture made,
You should have your clothes all on.
But mermaids, nymphs and fishes,
The myths of old declare,
Have no rules of etiquette,
So they have their pictures bare.

—Mona

The Park Villa in North Riverside Park owes its existence to a woman named Laura Ford Buckwalter. She lived a block away at 1106 Larimer Street and was a civic and political activist in the two decades preceding the passage of the women's suffrage amendment. She ran unsuccessfully for city commission in 1911, 1913, and 1918. (Courtesy Wichita Park Department.)

Laura Ford Buckwalter agitated for a public restroom for visitors to North Riverside Park who came to have picnics and see the various features, such as the Ross Fountain, Lily Pond, and Civil War cannon. The Riverside streetcar line ran just east of the site chosen for Park Villa. One of the streetcars is partially seen in this view from the southeast porch of Park Villa. (Courtesy Wichita Public Library, Local History Collection.)

HER WORK OF TWO YEARS DEDICATED

Laura Buckwalter is immortalized in the cornerstone of Park Villa, as is the local architect Ulysses Grant Charles who donated his services to design the building. Laura secured public subscriptions and donations of materials to get the building done. Prison labor was used at one point, and Laura actually stood guard over them. The city commission approved a bond issue of $3,851 on June 23, 1913, to repay her outstanding expenses.

Laura was photographed at the dedication for Park Villa on the evening of June 2, 1913. Two hundred people attended, and the speakers included Laura, U. G. Charles, and city commissioner R. B. Campbell. Commissioner John Harts was not in attendance; he had been quoted in the *Eagle* on March 23 as saying, "I would rather the Rest Room would have cost the taxpayers another $1,000 than to have had a woman build it." (Courtesy *Wichita Eagle*.)

The Lily Pond requires annual draining and cleaning to handle the accumulation of leaves and other organic debris at the bottom. Fish, turtles, and frogs are found occasionally during this procedure and are relocated. The large concrete pond in Oak Park needs similar regular maintenance. Workmen are seen here finishing up cleaning the Lily Pond in 1961. (Courtesy Wichita Park Department.)

In the recent renovations, subtly designed fountains were added in the form of metal lily sculptures, which have water dripping off their leaves. A low wrought-iron fence that previously surrounded the pond was removed, as was the street that formerly ran on the north side of Park Villa, reclaiming the interior of the park for pedestrians. A small parking lot was added for people using the facility.

Wichita approved a $39,000 bond issue in 1922 to purchase 23 acres of wooded land adjoining North Riverside Park. It was named Oak Park and considered a "sylvan paradise." The mature bur oak trees within it anchor a woodland habitat that draws large numbers of migrating warblers every spring. The sinuous unpaved drive that formerly wound through the park is now closed to cars. (Courtesy Wichita Park Department.)

Using water from a well and drawing inspiration from the natural landscapes of Kansas, L. W. Clapp designed an artificial stream in Oak Park leading to a series of lagoons. It was built in 1927 to 1928. The lower lagoon ended in a rocky grotto with a decorative arch constructed with limestone field rock from the Flint Hills east of Wichita. (Courtesy Wichita State University Library, Department of Special Collections.)

The lower lagoon in Oak Park did not have a concrete bottom and went dry when the well source for the stream was not able to keep up with the natural seepage into the ground. The bottom of the lagoon was sealed with bentonite during the recent Riverside Park renovations and water now sparkles there once again. Limestone ledges along the edge were added, as well as a new pedestrian bridge.

An 18-hole disc golf course was added to Oak Park in recent years. It has become a popular feature of the park. The fairways crisscross the meadows and forest edges and cross over into North Riverside Park. It is one of two disc golf courses in Wichita, with the other being in Herman Hill Park south of downtown. The Air Capital Disc Golf Club was established in 1989.

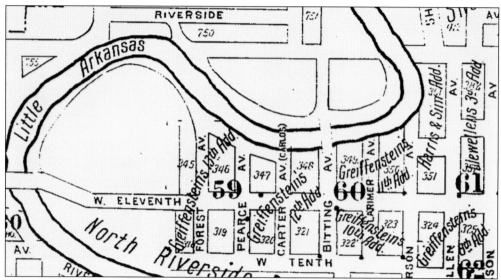

The Little River jumped its banks during the 1923 flood at the sharp bend south of Thirteenth Street. In 1924, the city cut another channel for the river to try to prevent a flood from occurring again, creating a new island. The Wichita Indians were asked to name it, and they christened it Mead Island in honor of James R. Mead, whom they still remembered and revered. (Courtesy the Sanborn Library LLC.)

In 1927, a group of Wichita Indians traveled to Wichita from Anadarko, Oklahoma, and constructed one of their traditional lodges on Mead Island. They brought all the materials needed with them, including the many bundles of slough grass necessary for the roof and the willow wands and long, narrow cedar poles used for the supporting framework. (Courtesy Wichita State University Library, Department of Special Collections.)

The lodge was built in only six days. During this time, the Wichitas stayed at the nearby tourist camp, located where Minisa Park is today. A temporary footbridge was built across the river for access to the island. The lodge had two doors, one facing east and the other facing west. The spires on top have a sacred purpose, pointing to the four cardinal directions and up. (Courtesy Wichita State University Library, Department of Special Collections.)

James R. Mead's widow, Fern Mead Jordan, is in this photograph along with Sook-a, the leader of the Wichita women that helped construct the lodge. The photograph was taken between June 7, when the lodge was completed, and June 9, when the Wichitas returned home. Sook-a had played in the woodlands of Riverside as a child when the tribe lived there during the Civil War, over 60 years before. (Courtesy Wichita State University Library, Department of Special Collections.)

A SCENE NEAR SULLIVAN'S DAM
WICHITA, KANSAS

In 1874, a dam was constructed on the Little Arkansas above town to divert water east to Chisholm Creek, where a gristmill had been built. The mill ceased operations by 1900. The city bought the dam and millrace in 1891. Arthur Sullivan, whose family had homesteaded land nearby, was hired to maintain it. It then became known as Sullivan's Dam. (Courtesy Wichita/Sedgwick County Historical Museum.)

This was the structure used to control the amount of water being diverted from Sullivan's Dam through the half-mile ditch connecting to the west fork of Chisholm Creek. Two packing plants were built on the west fork near Twenty-first and Broadway Streets in 1888, and the diverted water was given a new task—diluting and flushing away the offal from the packing plants. (Courtesy Wichita Public Library, Local History Collection.)

Walnut Grove was the name of a 17-acre park area just south of Thirty-ninth Street North along the impounded part of the Little River above Sullivan's Dam. It was owned and promoted by the Arkansas Valley Interurban, which had regular car service to it in the warm months. All traces of Sullivan's Dam and Walnut Grove were erased when a large flood-control diversion channel was constructed around Wichita in the 1950s.

Wichita's first air show happened at Walnut Grove from May 4–6, 1911. Here Eugene Ely pilots the first aircraft to take off at the meet, an early Curtiss biplane with a pusher prop engine. Also flying during the show were R. C. St. Henry, C. C. Witmer, and local favorite Jimmy Ward. Three generations of transportation technology are visible in this photograph: horses, automobiles, and airplanes. (Courtesy Wichita State University Library, Department of Special Collections.)

May 4, 5, 6, 1911
Walnut Grove Station

On the Arkansas Valley
Interurban Railway

WICHITA'S FIRST
AVIATION MEET

Pass _E. T. Battin + Wife_

TO GROUNDS AND GRAND STAND OR AUTO BOX

Account _City Commissioner_

Nº   3   _O A Boyle_
                                Manager

Edmundson Taylor Battin and his wife received this pass to the 1911 air show at Walnut Grove. He was a city commissioner at the time, so one would expect complimentary treatment for local officials, but he was also on the board of the Arkansas Valley Interurban. The disclaimer wording on the backside of the pass demonstrates that liability worries for event promoters are not a recent phenomenon. (Both courtesy Wichita/Sedgwick County Historical Museum.)

IMPORTANT

This ticket is issued upon the express condition and understanding that the holder hereby absolves The Curtiss Exhibition Co., O. A. Boyle, Local Manager, and their agents and employees from any and all liability for any injury which the holder may sustain from any Aeroplane or parts thereof. The holder of this ticket agrees that his admission to the grounds upon this ticket shall be conclusive evidence of his consent to the above condition, which is part of the contract of admission.

Seven

RECENT TIMES IN THE RIVERSIDE PARKS

Wichita rediscovered its rivers in a big way beginning in 1970, when a yearlong celebration of the town's centennial concluded with the Wichitennial Water Festival on the river. That proved to be very popular, and plans were laid to have something similar on an annual basis. The first Wichitennial River Festival was in 1972 and has since grown into a full 10 days of merrymaking. The name was shortened in 1979 to the Wichita River Festival. For many years, a flyover by aircraft from nearby McConnell Air Force Base was a featured part of the final day's activities. The planes in the flyover depended on what was stationed at the base that year. F-4 Phantom fighters, seen here, were used in the 1980s, as were B-1 bombers. These planes always surprised the thousands gathered downtown by sneaking in "on the deck," where they could not be seen or heard coming, and lighting their afterburners just before they roared overhead. (Courtesy *Wichita Eagle*.)

The official ambassador for the River Festival is Admiral Windwagon Smith, a fictional character derived from early inventors who attempted to use sails to drive wagons on the prairie. A different person is chosen to be the admiral each year. In 1980, it was Tom Allen, who was director of the park department for many years. He is seen here waving to the crowd on the riverbank at one of the festival's aquatic events. (Courtesy Wichita Festivals Inc.)

Harkening back to the balloon race on Ackerman's Island in 1915, a balloon liftoff was a featured event at several festivals. Unlike their predecessors, the modern balloons used hot air rather than natural gas for inflation. But in some years, the event could not be held because the winds were too strong. Sim Park was the site of this liftoff. (Courtesy *Wichita Eagle*.)

106

A wide variety of not-so-serious competitive events are a part of the River Festival. One popular river-based contest is a bathtub race. Each entry must include an old cast-iron bathtub, but beyond that designs range from sophisticated to preposterous, such as this entry. Another event called "Bedlam" involved wheeled hospital beds being pushed along a blocked-off street. (Courtesy *Wichita Eagle*.)

Bicycle races have been a part of the River Festival most years; usually they have been held in one of the Riverside Parks. A loop course around Central Riverside Park was used until the mid-1980s, when the extension of Wiley Street through the park was removed. Different classes of racers competed against each other, culminating in the grueling 40-mile professional event. Here an amateur class rounds the bend by the Murdock Bridge. (Courtesy Wichita Festivals Inc.)

Admission for each year's festival is obtained by purchasing a button to wear while attending events. This mirrors how admission was handled for the fall fairs that were held on the downtown streets in the early 1900s. Along with each year's button, the same artist also produces a unique poster. These two photographs show every button from 1973 through to 2010. The buttons are

mostly of the same size and format, but there are some exceptions: 1996 was the 25th year and a second, limited-edition large button was also produced; 1993 had a rectangular button; 1975 and 1976 offered pins shaped like wind wagons instead of buttons; and 2007 had four slightly different buttons.

The grand finale of each year's festival is a large display of fireworks along the Arkansas River. A nationally recognized pyrotechnics firm in Wichita specializes in displays choreographed with music. A local radio station carries the music, and people bring portable radios so the sound is evenly dispersed throughout the crowd. The founder of the firm, Paul Austin, is seen here making preparations for the 1985 show. (Courtesy *Wichita Eagle*.)

The Douglas Avenue Bridge was completely re-decked in 1999, and the River Festival was an important factor in its design. The new bridge has double-tiered viewing areas on both the upstream and downstream sidewalks to accommodate observation of the river by pedestrians. Large ornamental features made of metal tubing were also added, suggestive of the sails on Admiral Smith's wind wagon.

A. Price Woodard Jr. Park is along the east bank of the Arkansas River just south of the Douglas Bridge. The park is named for a former city commissioner and mayor. It was completed in the 1970s, in the early years of the River Festival. It has an amphitheater facing the river, an ideal spot for watching the festival fireworks. Harry Bertoia's metal sculpture *Interrupted Flight* tops a grassy rise.

Wichita began building bicycle paths along the Arkansas River in the 1960s. They have been added to over the years and now extend virtually the entire length of the river within the city. There are paths on both sides of the river along most of the stretch through downtown. The entire bicycle path network in Wichita has grown to over 100 miles.

On Saturday, May 22, 1965, a new park was dedicated on the west bank of the Arkansas River three miles south of downtown. It encompasses 119 acres, over 40 of which are lakes formed by former sandpits. The park was named in honor of O. J. Watson, who served on the Board of Park Commisioners from 1927 to 1963. He was 89 when he attended the grand opening. (Courtesy Wichita Park Department.)

O. J. Watson Park offers many recreational opportunities for Wichita. It not only has fishing and picnicking, but also boat rentals, pony rides, miniature golf, and a miniature train. The bicycle path along the river connects to the park. Every year around Halloween, a haunted island feature is created in the middle of the north lake. (Courtesy Wichita Park Department.)

For over three decades, Watson Park was entered on the east side via Old Lawrence Road, a street that was once the route for U.S. 81 Highway and still has its original brick paving from the early 1900s. Recently a new entrance was created on the west side of the park on South McLean Boulevard. The metal cattail sculptures evoke the aquatic features in the park.

The Wichita Area Treatment and Remediation (WATER) Center is in Herman Hill Park on the north bank of the Arkansas River across from Watson Park. The award-winning facility combines a treatment center for groundwater pollution, a water park, and a public education program on all aspects of water including the nearby river. The innovative architectural design incorporates sculpture, cascading water features, and a large outdoor aquarium.

Botanica, the Wichita Gardens, is located between Sim Park and Old Cowtown. It opened in 1987 and has over 20 themed gardens on nine acres of land. Thousands of visitors every year enjoy this beautiful spot in the city. Two buildings on the grounds were constructed in 1921 with recycled streetcar paver stones; the buildings were once the golf course clubhouse and a station for the Arkansas Valley Interurban.

The South Riverside Park Tennis Center was built on the site where the Municipal Beach swimming pool was formerly located. It opened in 1976 and has 14 courts and a handball practice wall. The building was renamed in honor of former city manager Ralph Wulz in 1988. In 1921, the first tennis courts in the Wichita parks were constructed where the east parking lot for the tennis center is now.

Veterans Memorial Park is on the east bank of the Arkansas River across from Exploration Place. The Korean War Memorial seen here is one of several features in the park. The park also includes memorials to the merchant marine, Marine Corps, Vietnam veterans, Pearl Harbor, combat-wounded veterans, and World War II submarine veterans.

The USS *Wichita* was a heavy cruiser built in the Philadelphia Navy Yard. In 1935, its keel was laid; the vessel was completed in 1937 and commissioned in 1939. It served in both the Atlantic and Pacific fleets, but it was decommissioned in 1947, and then scrapped in 1959. This unique limestone depiction of the ship's profile is in Veterans Memorial Park along the riverbank.

Kiowa-Comanche artist Blackbear Bosin designed this monumental sculpture, the *Keeper of the Plains*. It was placed at the junction of the Arkansas and Little Arkansas Rivers and dedicated May 18, 1974. The sculpture is 44 feet tall and executed in Cor-Ten steel, which naturally weathers to a deep reddish-brown. (Courtesy Wichita Festivals Inc.)

Blackbear Bosin had a long career as a graphic designer at the Boeing plant in Wichita. While the *Keeper of the Plains* is his most widely recognized work, he was primarily a painter. He also did a long, multi-panel tile mosaic on the history of Wichita that graces the walls in the downstairs ballroom of the Broadview Hotel. (Courtesy Wichita Festivals Inc.)

On March 8, 1975, the ground-breaking ceremony was held for the Mid-America All-Indian Center, located just behind the *Keeper of the Plains*. Participating were Governor Robert Bennett (light-colored hat) and Mayor Garry Porter, seen here just to the left of Winnebago elder Jay Hunter, who later became the facility's executive director. The center was designated as one of 150 national bicentennial projects. (Courtesy Wichita Festivals Inc.)

The Mid-America All-Indian Center houses a museum and hosts frequent powwows. Flags from over 70 Native American nations hang from the ceiling of the large Kiva Ceremonial Hall in the middle of the building. Known as the Gallery of Nations, it has the goal of displaying the flags from all 549 recognized nations.

In 2006, the *Keeper of the Plains* was elevated on a 30-foot pedestal and connected to both riverbanks with strikingly designed pedestrian bridges. The bridges resemble bows drawn back with arrows ready to shoot. The landscaping on both riverbanks was extensively modified with gardens, uniquely designed benches, and native plantings. The area around the base of the statue includes interpretive displays about the Plains Indians. Fire pots located on large rocks in the river below the statue are lit on calm nights.

The design team for the new riverbank landscaping was challenged by what to do with a large concrete storm sewer on the east bank. Formerly the outfall structure for the cooling water drawn from the river for the nearby electric power plant, it was so massive it would have been very expensive to tear out. But it still flowed after rains, so it had an ongoing purpose and could not be done away with entirely. Somebody commented that it looked like a troll's cave, so one was created for it. The troll lurks beneath a metal grate and is illuminated by green lights after dark.

A sinuous row of cages was built along Nims Street at the Central Riverside Park Zoo in 1960. It was all that remained after 1972, along with the two waterfowl ponds and the alligator pit (which was filled in with soil and repurposed as a prairie dog exhibit). By the early 1980s, rust and rot had taken its toll on the cage structure, and it needed repair or replacement. (Courtesy Wichita Park Department.)

In 1985, the park department said it was contemplating eliminating the zoo, provoking a loud chorus of opposition from Wichitans, many of who were once taken there by their grandparents when they were children. The decision was made to build a new facility, and the site chosen was the same spot where the Park Zoo and Lion House had once been.

The first animal obtained for the new facility was an orphan beaver kit found near the Arkansas River. The beaver's name was Webster (although it was realized later the name should be Webster Sue). Webster met thousands of people in outreach programs, helping them become better acquainted with Kansas's native wildlife. Webster buttons and T-shirts were sold to raise funds for the renovation and to promote awareness of the new facility.

During the transition phase, this unique button was donated to park staff by a local resident. Its age and purpose are not known, but one can presume it was made for much the same reason the Webster buttons were—to promote awareness of the zoo. The modest clothing of the chimpanzees is notable, as is the mimed message of "Hear no evil; Speak no evil; See no evil."

During the grand-opening weekend for the Kansas Wildlife Exhibit on October 29 and 30, 1988, Webster the beaver was a featured program animal, along with several other residents of the new display. Here Bob Gress and Connie Hay present Webster and one of the other beavers. Schoolchildren from nearby Riverside Elementary School came earlier in the week in their Halloween costumes for cake and ice cream at a picnic sponsored by the local Wendy's franchise.

The Kansas Wildlife Exhibit was constructed on the same site where the Lion House, Park Zoo, and ostrich pen were once located. The new zoo features only Kansas-native animals. The extension of Wiley Street through the park was removed, and a parking lot was added next to the Pagoda. This sign greeted visitors coming from that lot; both the sign and the lot were removed in 2002.

This 2008 aerial photograph shows the current layout of Central Riverside Park, including the new half-mile oval walking path, the new roundabouts at the Murdock Street and Nims Street entrances, and the two new ponds. The large evergreen trees located to the north and east of the central pond appear much darker in this afternoon wintertime shot. They date to the early 1900s, and their positions show where the original racetrack oval was located. (Courtesy City of Wichita Geographic Information Services.)

A new feature in Central Riverside Park is a monumental solar calendar, located in the north half of the park. Designed by local artist Steve Murillo, it has large limestone rocks aligned to mark the equinoxes and solstices. Mosaic tile murals on the rocks interpret the night sky.

This large copper-roofed gazebo is another recent addition to the park, echoing the bandstand built nearby in 1899. A large pond was created in the middle of the park next to the new gazebo. Metal lily pad sculptures float within the pond, and a plaza was added on the west side of the pond overlooking it.

Public swimming facilities were located along the Little Arkansas River west of Nims in 1917.

A new half-mile oval walking path circles within Central Riverside Park, with a different shape and alignment compared to the original one in Davidson's Park. The history of Riverside is noted in 12 ground-level markers that are seen along the new path. Each features a photograph of an historic feature in the area and a short caption explaining its significance.

A water play area was added to Central Riverside Park, offering a fun place for kids of all ages to cool off in summer. It is centrally located in relation to all the other features in the park. Sidewalks branch out toward the zoo, playground, Pagoda, and the new lake by the gazebo pavilion.

One of the sidewalks branching from the water play area leads to the Kansas Wildlife Exhibit, which continues a zoo tradition in Central Riverside Park that began in 1901. The recent renovations to Wichita's Riverside Parks have restored and extended their appeal as they progress through their second century of existence. They remain a vital part of the city's social and recreational life.

BIBLIOGRAPHY

Bentley, Orsemus H. *History of Wichita and Sedgwick County Kansas*, Chicago: C. F. Cooper & Company, 1910.

Dr. Edward N. Tihen's Notes from Wichita Newspapers. Special Collections and University Archives, Wichita State University Libraries. http://special collections.wichita.edu/collections/local_history/tihen/index.asp

Goodrum, Charles A. *I'll Trade You an Elk*, New York: Funk & Wagnalls, 1967.

Henline, Beverly A. *In the Whirligig of Time: Pages from Wichita History*, Wichita, KS: Wichita-Sedgwick County Historical Museum Association, 1995.

Kirkman, Kay. *Wichita, A Pictorial History*, Norfolk, VA: The Donning Company, 1981.

Lewis, Will G. *The Good Old Days, Wichita, 1890–1900*. Wichita, KS: Community Press, 1969.

Long, Richard M. *Wichita Century*, Wichita, KS: Wichita Historical Museum Association, Inc., 1969.

Mead, James R. *Hunting and Trading on the Great Plains 1859–1875*, Wichita, KS: Rowfant Press, 2008.

Miner, Craig. *Wichita: The Early Years, 1865–80*, Lincoln, NE: University of Nebraska, 1982.

———. *Wichita: The Magic City*, Wichita, KS: Wichita-Sedgwick County Historical Museum Association, 1988.

Peerless Princess of the Plains: Postcard Views of Early Wichita, Wichita, KS: Two Rivers Publishing Co., 1976.

Pratt, George B. *"The Magic City": Wichita, Picturesque and Descriptive*. Neenah, WI: Art Publishing Co., 1889.

Price, Jay M. *Wichita 1865–1930*, Charleston, SC: Arcadia Publishing, 2003.

INDEX

Ackerman's Island, 73, 74, 80, 81
Alligators, 38, 50, 52, 54–56, 120
A. Price Woodard Park, 111
Art Museum, 16, 87, 91, 92
Balloons, 80, 106
Bicycles in the parks, 26, 107, 111, 112
Boating on the river, 18, 24, 25, 31, 32, 57–61, 87
Bosin, Blackbear, 116
Botanica, 114
Boy With a Boot fountain, 27, 33, 66
Buckwalter, Laura, 95, 96
Buttons, 64, 108, 109, 121
Cannons, 27, 33, 34, 39, 45, 70, 95
Central Riverside Park, 12, 19, 25, 26, 37–72, 107, 120–125
Chisholm Trail, 14
Circuses in the parks, 22, 26, 45
Clapp. L. W., 34, 48, 72, 84, 98
Davidson, J. O., 20–23, 35, 48
Delano, 15
Douglas Bridge, 14–16, 74, 110, 111
Exploration Place, 82, 115
Gay, George and Lucy, 17, 18
Griswold's Park, 17
Hartzell, John Wesley, 17
Herman Hill Park, 99, 113
Hiker Statue, 70, 71
Island Park, 78–80, 83
Keeper of the Plains, 16, 31, 116–118
Lawrence–Dumont Stadium, 78, 83
Lily Pond, 33, 36, 93–95, 97

McLean, Ben, 82
Mead Island, 100, 101
Mead, James R., 11, 12, 93, 100, 101
Mid–America All–Indian Center, 91, 117
Munger House, 12, 13, 85
Municipal Beach, 87–91, 114
North Riverside Park, 27, 29, 33–36, 86
O. J. Watson Park, 112, 113
Oak Park, 97–99
Old Cowtown, 16, 85, 114
Pagoda Building, 52, 68, 72, 122, 125
Park Villa, 33, 36, 95–97
River Festival, 105–111
Riverside Boat House, 46, 57–61, 63, 65
Riverside Club, 86
Ross, Finlay, 27, 28, 36, 47, 63, 70
Shuman's Grove, 17, 18
Sim Park, 28, 84, 106, 114
Sim, Coler, 28, 84
South Riverside Park, 16–18, 26, 30, 32, 38, 87–93, 114
Spanish American War Memorial, 70, 71
Streetcars, 21–24, 30, 37, 38, 44, 46–48, 62, 72, 76, 86, 91, 95–114
Sullivan's Dam, 102, 103
Tennis Center, 114
Troll, 119
Veterans Memorial Park, 115
Walnut Grove, 103, 104
WATER Center, 113
Wonderland Park, 73–78, 82
Zoo, 37–56, 72, 120–125

www.arcadiapublishing.com

Discover books about the town where you grew up, the cities where your friends and families live, the town where your parents met, or even that retirement spot you've been dreaming about. Our Web site provides history lovers with exclusive deals, advanced notification about new titles, e-mail alerts of author events, and much more.

MADE IN THE USA

Arcadia Publishing, the leading local history publisher in the United States, is committed to making history accessible and meaningful through publishing books that celebrate and preserve the heritage of America's people and places. Consistent with our mission to preserve history on a local level, this book was printed in South Carolina on American-made paper and manufactured entirely in the United States.

This book carries the accredited Forest Stewardship Council (FSC) label and is printed on 100 percent FSC-certified paper. Products carrying the FSC label are independently certified to assure consumers that they come from forests that are managed to meet the social, economic, and ecological needs of present and future generations.

FSC
Mixed Sources
Product group from well-managed
forests and other controlled sources

Cert no. SW-COC-001530
www.fsc.org
© 1996 Forest Stewardship Council

Find Your Place in History.